Sign Language & Colors

Bela Davis

Abdo Kids Junior
is an Imprint of Abdo Kids
abdobooks.com

Abdo
EVERYDAY SIGN LANGUAGE
Kids

abdobooks.com

Published by Abdo Kids, a division of ABDO, P.O. Box 398166, Minneapolis, Minnesota 55439.
Copyright © 2022 by Abdo Consulting Group, Inc. International copyrights reserved in all countries.
No part of this book may be reproduced in any form without written permission from the publisher.
Abdo Kids Junior™ is a trademark and logo of Abdo Kids.

Printed in the United States of America, North Mankato, Minnesota.

052021

092021

 THIS BOOK CONTAINS RECYCLED MATERIALS

Photo Credits: iStock, Shutterstock

Production Contributors: Teddy Borth, Jennie Forsberg, Grace Hansen

Design Contributors: Candice Keimig, Pakou Moua

Library of Congress Control Number: 2020947499

Publisher's Cataloging-in-Publication Data

Names: Davis, Bela, author.

Title: Sign language & colors / by Bela Davis

Description: Minneapolis, Minnesota : Abdo Kids, 2022 | Series: Everyday sign language | Includes online resources and index.

Identifiers: ISBN 9781098206994 (lib. bdg.) | ISBN 9781098207830 (ebook) | ISBN 9781098208257 (Read-to-Me ebook)

Subjects: LCSH: American Sign Language--Juvenile literature. | Colors--Juvenile literature. | Rainbows--Juvenile literature. | Deaf--Means of communication--Juvenile literature. | Language acquisition--Juvenile literature.

Classification: DDC 419--dc23

Table of Contents

Signs and Colors

ASL is a visual language.

There is a sign for every color!

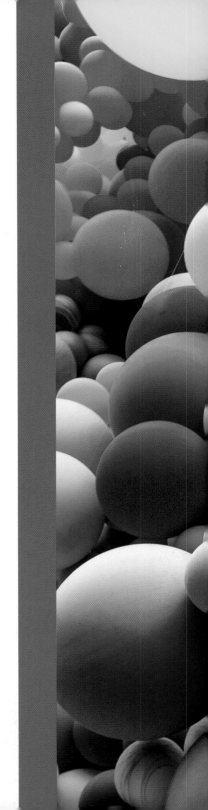

4

COLOR

1. Bring one open hand to chin, palm toward face

2. Wiggle fingers on chin

5

Lisa's mittens and hat are blue!

Her gift is blue too!

BLUE

1. Make the "B" sign
2. Twist hand back and forth

Max has an ice cream cone.

It is pink and yummy.

PINK

1. Make the "P" sign
2. Tap lips with the inside of the middle finger and brush downward a couple of times

9

Andy has a green inner tube.

He is ready for the pool!

GREEN

1. Make the "G" sign
2. Twist hand back and forth

11

Lea loves costumes. She is a big, orange pumpkin!

12

ORANGE

1. Place hand near chin

2. Repeatedly move hand in and out of a fist

3. It should look like you are squeezing an orange!

Louie has a red bow tie.

He feels fancy.

RED

1. Point to lips with pointer finger
2. Brush finger down chin

15

Max has a new shirt.

It is white.

WHITE

1. Bring hand to middle of chest

2. With open hand, touch all fingertips to chest

3. Bring hand away from chest a few inches while pulling fingertips together

17

It's a rainy day. Sam is
ready in his yellow outfit.

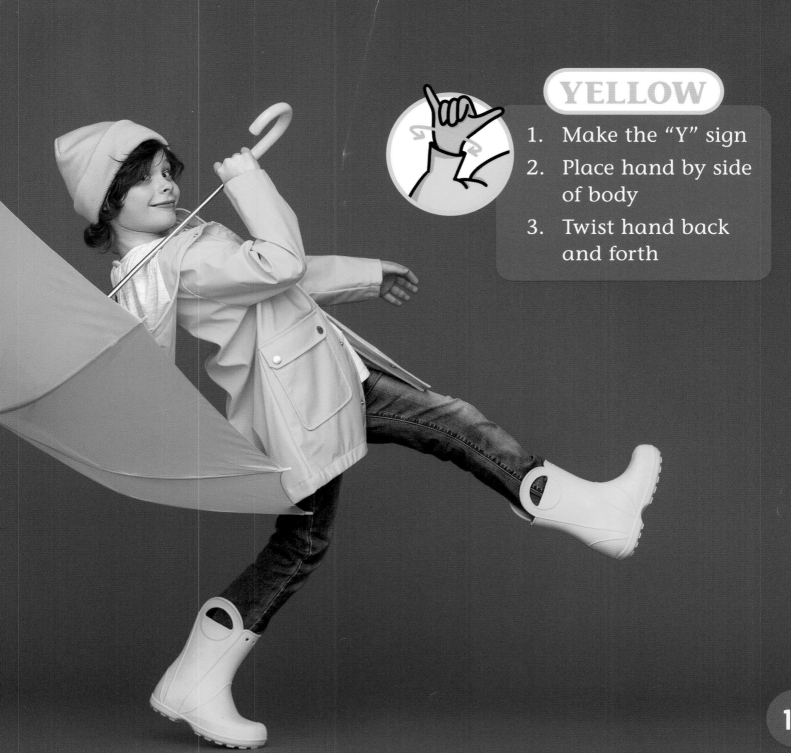

YELLOW

1. Make the "Y" sign
2. Place hand by side of body
3. Twist hand back and forth

19

Mimi's favorite color is purple.

Her hijab has purple in it.

PURPLE

1. Make the "P" sign
2. Twist hand back and forth

21

The ASL Alphabet!

Glossary

I LOVE YOU · HELLO · FRIEND · MOTHER · FATHER · BABY · YES · NO · PLEASE · BATHROOM · THANK YOU · SCHOOL

ASL
short for American Sign Language, a language used by many deaf people in North America.

costume
clothing worn to make one look like some other person, animal, or thing.

hijab
a cloth that covers the head, hair, and neck of some Muslim women.

Index

Abdo Kids
ONLINE
FREE! ONLINE MULTIMEDIA RESOURCES

Visit **abdokids.com** to access crafts, games, videos, and more!

Use Abdo Kids code
ESK6994
or scan this QR code!